LET'S HAVE A PARTY!

Illustrated by
Ronald Fritz

Troll Associates

LIBRARY OF CONGRESS CATALOGING-IN-PUBLICATION DATA
Let's have a party! / illustrated by Ron Fritz.
p. of music. — (Troll singalongs)
Children's songs by or arr. by Dennis Scott.
With piano acc.; includes chord symbols.
Summary: Fourteen songs suitable for singing at parties, including
"The Hokey Pokey," "Bingo Limbo," and "Head, Shoulders, Knees, and
Toes."
ISBN 0-8167-2984-0 (lib. bdg.)   ISBN 0-8167-2985-9 (pbk.)
1. Children's songs.   [1. Songs.]   I. Fritz, Ronald, ill.
II. Scott, Dennis.   III. Series.
M1997.L576   1993   92-28560

Published by Troll Associates
Words and music for "Welcome to the Party" by Dennis Scott
Original arrangements for all other titles by Dennis Scott

Text copyright © 1993 Troll Associates

Illustration copyright © 1993 Ronald Fritz

The publisher wishes to thank Randa Kirshbaum for her transcriptions
of these original musical arrangements.

Printed in the United States of America
10 9 8 7 6 5 4 3 2 1

Contents

Welcome to the Party!

Fast rhythm and blues

Words and Music by Dennis Scott

Wel - come to the par - ty, wel - come to the fun.

Wel - come to the par - ty, come on, ev - 'ry- one. We've

got a lot of things we wan - na do. And we

can't have a par - ty with - out you.

2. Welcome to the party, welcome to the fun.
   Welcome to the party, come on everyone.
   And party time is always something new.
   And we can't have a party without you.

Spoken Chorus:

   We're gonna clap our hands — jump and run —
   Shake our heads — stick out our tongue —
   Sing out loud — roll on the floor —
   Just go crazy, that's what a party's for.

3. … you'll be laughing right along before we're through,…

5

The Hokey Pokey

turn your-self a-round, and that's what it's all a - bout. 5. You put your

Hoedown
2. Everybody circle to the right,…
3. Everybody clap your hands,…

Drawl
5. You put your left foot in,…
6. You put your right shoulder in,…

Hoedown
7. Everybody circle to the left,…
8. Everybody swing your partner,…
   … everybody stop in place.

Drawl, modulate to G
9. You put your head in,…
10. You put your bellybutton in,…
11. You put your backside in,…
    … listen carefully.
12. You put your whole self out,…

She'll Be Coming 'Round the Mountain

Slow old timey harmony

Arranged by Dennis Scott

2. She'll be driving six white horses when she comes.
She'll be driving six white horses when she comes.
She'll be driving six white horses,
She'll be driving six white horses,
She'll be driving six white horses when she comes!
(Whoa, back, toot, toot)

3. Oh, we'll all go out to meet her when she comes,...
(Hi, Babe, whoa, back, toot, toot)

Modulate to E

4. Oh, we'll give the dog a bath when she comes,...
(Arf, arf, hi, Babe, whoa, back, toot, toot)

5. Oh, we'll take her out for pizza when she comes,...
(Yum, yum, etc.)

Modulate to F

6. She'll wear polka dot pajamas when she comes,...
(Whistle, whistle, etc.)

Modulate to G flat

7. She'll be coming 'round the mountain when
she comes,...

9

I Am a Fine Musician

Arranged by Dennis Scott

2. I am a fine musician, I come from
   Zanzibar.
   And people love to hear me play my songs
   on my guitar.
   Du du du du du, du du du du du, du du du
   du du du du.
   Skipping and playing, singing and swaying.
   Du du du du du,...

3. I am a fine musician, Paree is where
   I've been.
   And people there just love to hear me play
   my violin.
   Fiddle fiddle fiddle fiddle,...

Modulate to E flat

4. I am a fine musician and London that's
   me roots.
   And people love to hear me play upon me
   silver flute.
   Dida di di di,...

5. We all are fine musicians, we practice
   every day.
   And people come from miles around just to
   hear us play.
   (Child plays his own instrument)

11

If You're Happy

Arranged by Dennis Scott

If you're hap - py and you know it clap your hands. *(Clap   clap)* If you're

hap - py and you know it clap your hands. *(Clap   clap)* If you're

hap - py and you know it, then you real - ly got - ta show it. If you're

hap - py and you know it clap your hands. *(Clap   clap)*

2. If you're happy and you know it stomp your feet.
   If you're happy and you know it stomp your feet.
   If you're happy and you know it, then you really
     gotta show it.
   If you're happy and you know it stomp your feet.

3. ... blow a kiss,...

4. ... shake your head,...

Modulate to F

5. ... shout out loud,...

6. ... dance around,...

Modulate to E

7. Put your finger in the air, in the air.
   Put your finger in the air, in the air.
   Put your finger in the air, so we can see that it
     is there.
   Put your finger in the air, in the air.

8. Put your finger on your nose, on your nose,...
   Put your finger on your nose, that's where the
     wind blows,...

9. Put your finger in your ear, in your ear,...
   Put your finger in your ear, keep it there for
     'bout a year,...

Repeat verse 1

13

Going to Kentucky

Arranged by Dennis Scott

Rocking

Verse

G   A

We're go - ing to Ken - tuck - y. We're go - ing to the fair, to

D   D 7   G   *Chorus*
                                        D 7(6)

see a se - ño - ri - ta with flow - ers in her hair. Oh,

G   A   D

shake it, shake it, shake it, shake it all you can. Shake it like a milk-shake, and

14

do it once a-gain. Oh, rum - ble to the bot - tom, rum - ble to the top,

turn a - round and turn a - round un - til you make a stop!

2. We're going to Virginia.
   We're going to the fair,
   to buy a cow named Bessie
   and sell the old gray mare.

Chorus
Modulate to A flat

3. We're going to Hawaii.
   We're going to the fair,
   to learn to do the hoola
   in our underwear.

Chorus

Old MacDonald

Start each verse with, "New MacDonald had a farm,..."

2. And on that farm he had a helicopter,...

3. And on that farm he had a computer,...

4. And on that farm he had a spaceship,...

5. And on that farm he had a race car,...

6. And on that farm he had some ghosts,...

17

Knees Up, Mother Brown

knees up, knees up, nev-er let the breeze up, knees up, Moth-er Brown.

2. Hopping on one foot, hopping on one foot,
hopping, hopping, never stopping,
hopping on one foot.

3. Hopping on the other,…
hopping, hopping, never stopping,…

4. Standing on your head,…
standing, standing, how demanding,…

Repeat Verse 1

5. Twirling all around,…
twirling, twirling, never swirling,…

Modulate to B

6. Twisting all around,…
twisting, twisting, always twisting,…

7. Twisting to the ground,…
lower, lower, don't get slower,…

Repeat Verse 1

Bingo Limbo

Limbo beat

Arranged by Dennis Scott

There was a far - mer had a dog, and Bin - go was his name - o.

B - I - N - G - O, B - I - N - G - O, B - I -

N - G - O, and Bin - go was his name - o.   *Lower the limbo pole.*

2. There was a farmer had a dog,
   and Bingo was his name-o.
   Clap-I-N-G-O, *Clap*-I-N-G-O,
   Clap-I-N-G-O, and Bingo was his name-o.

3. There was a farmer had a dog,…
   Clap-Clap-N-G-O, *Clap-Clap*-N-G-O,…

Modulate to F

4. There was a farmer had a dog,…
   Clap-Clap-Clap-G-O, *Clap-Clap-Clap*-G-O,…

5. There was a farmer had a dog,…
   Clap-Clap-Clap-Clap-O, *Clap-Clap-Clap-Clap*-O,…

6. There was a farmer had a dog,…
   Clap-Clap-Clap-Clap-Clap, *Clap-Clap-Clap-Clap-Clap*,…

Green Grass

Fast, hillbilly

Arranged by Dennis Scott

There was a tree, *there was a tree,* a pret-ty lit-tle tree, *a pret-ty lit-tle*

tree, the pret-ti-est tree, *the pret-ti-est tree,* that you ev-er did see, *that you ev-er did*

see. And the tree in a hole, and the hole in the ground, and the

repeat music for v. 2-8

green grass grew all a-round, all a-round, the green grass grew all a-round.

2. Now on this tree, there was a limb,
   the longest limb, that you ever did see.
   And the limb on the tree,
   and the tree in a hole,
   and the hole in the ground,
   and the green grass grew all around, all around,
   the green grass grew all around.

3. Now on this limb, there was a branch,
   the biggest branch,...

Modulate to E

4. Now on this branch, there was a twig,
   the tiniest twig,...

5. Now on this twig, there was a leaf,
   the loveliest leaf,...

6. Now on this leaf, there was a nest,
   the fluffiest nest,...

Modulate to F

7. Now in this nest, there was an egg,
   the bluest egg,...

8. We could go on, and on and on,
   but this old yarn, is too far gone.
   And the green grass grew all around, all around,
   the green grass grew all around.

23

Mama Don't Allow

Up-tempo country

Arranged by Dennis Scott

Ma - ma don't al - low no ban - jo play - in' here.

Ma - ma don't al - low no ban - jo play - in' here. Well,

I don't care what Ma - ma don't al - low, gon - na play my ban - jo an - y - how.

Ma - ma don't al - low no ban - jo play - in' here.

2. Mama don't allow no piano playin' here.
Mama don't allow no piano playin' here.
Well, I don't care what Mama don't allow,
gonna play my piano anyhow.
Mama don't allow no piano playin' here.

Modulate to D flat

3. Mama don't allow no bass playin' here,…
Well, I don't care what Mama don't allow,
gonna slap that bass anyhow,…

Modulate to D

4. Mama don't allow no guitar playin' here,…
Well, I don't care what Mama don't allow,
gonna play my guitar anyhow,…

Modulate to E flat

5. Mama don't allow no sing-along singin' here,…
Well, I don't care what Mama don't allow,
gonna sing my songs anyhow,…

Bumblebee

Arranged by Dennis Scott

Simple

I'm bring-ing home a ba - by bum-ble-bee. Won't my mom-my

be so proud of me! I'm bring-ing home a ba - by bum-ble-bee.

Ouch! It stung me! *after Verse 4 only* B - U - M -

B - L - E There is no bum-ble-bee on me!

2. I'm squashing up my baby bumblebee.
   Won't my mommy be so proud of me?
   I'm squashing up my baby bumblebee.
   Ooh! It's all over me!

   Modulate to G flat

3. I'm wiping off my baby bumblebee.
   Won't my mommy be so proud of me?
   I'm wiping off my baby bumblebee.
   Look! It's off me!

4. *"Buzz" the melody of the last verse.*

Head, Shoulders, Knees, and Toes

Lively

Arranged by Dennis Scott

Head, shoul-ders, knees and toes, knees and toes,

head, shoul-ders, knees and toes, knees and toes,— and—

eyes and ears and mouth— and— nose.

Head, shoul-ders, knees and toes, knees and toes.

Every time you repeat a chorus, point to the part of the body that is mentioned, rather than saying its name, beginning with the word "head."

Boom, Boom, Ain't It Great to Be Crazy

Bouncy

Arranged by Dennis Scott

A horse and a flea and the three blind mice sat on a curb-stone shoot-ing dice. The horse, he slipped and fell on the flea. "Whoops," said the flea, "there's a horse on me!" Boom, boom, ain't it great to be cra-zy? Boom, boom, ain't it great to be cra-zy? Gid-dy and fool-ish the

whole day through. Boom, boom, ain't it great to be cra - zy?

2. Way down South where bananas grow,
   a flea stepped on an elephant's toe.
   The elephant cried with the tears in his eyes,
   "Why don't you pick on someone your size?"

Chorus

Modulate to F

3. Way up North where there's ice and snow,
   there lived a penguin and his name was Joe.
   He got so tired of black and white,
   he wore pink slacks to the dance last night.

Chorus